Devon Rex Cats and Kittens

Everything About Acquisition, Care, Nutrition, Behavior, Personality, Health, Training and more (Cat Owner's Books)

Clare Smiley

Copyright and Trademarks

Disclaimer and Legal Notice

consult with his or her own advisor before putting any of the enclosed information, ideas, or practices written in this book in to practice. .

Dedicated to our two wonderful cats
brother and sister - 'Kevin and Lucy'
(they were called that before we acquired them in 2000)

Contents

Contents

Introduction

Thank you for buying this book.

You are about to discover proven steps and methods on how to **select and raise a beautiful Devon Rex cat as a loving companion.**

I'll show you how you can train your little bundle of playful fun! They are loving and energetic but will also happily cuddle up to you. In my opinion they are the perfect cats. If you love the companionship, you will love learning more about the pixie of the cat world, the Devon Rex!

Learn more about its humble origins, its playful personality and how it can fit into your home to become a loving, faithful cat companion. By the time you finish reading this book, you will want one of these beautiful creatures in your home to love and adore.

Chapter 1 - The Origins of the Devon Rex

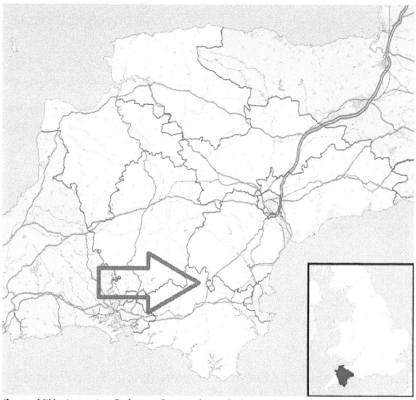

(Image Nilfanion, using Ordnance Survey data - Ordnance Survey OpenData)

Their large ears and eyes give them a distinctive look prized by their owners while their short, wavy sleek fur makes their bodies look as if they are hairless.

At first glance, the Devon Rex is easily confused with the Sphynx. Although the Sphynx is hairless, both breeds share a triangular shaped head, large ears, prominent cheekbones and large eyes. The Devon Rex is often referred to as the "pixies of the cat world" for their appearance and playful nature.

From Where?

This cat breed was discovered in Buckfastleigh, Devon, England in 1960 when a cat with short, curly fur was found by a closed tin mine. The Englishwoman who found the cat, Beryl Cox, was hoping to breed him, but she was never able to catch that particular cat. Instead, after he had bred with a stray female cat, Ms. Cox was able to befriend her.

Ms. Cox lived near the tin mine and one day she discovered that the female had a litter of kittens near the back of her garden. One of the kittens, a tiny male, had his father's distinctive curly fur, so she took him in and cared for the kitten that she named Kirlee. Kirlee eventually fathered the Devon Rex cat breed when Ms. Cox contacted a nearby group of breeders who owned a Cornish Rex.

The Cornish Rex was a breed that had been discovered just 10 years earlier in England. The group wanted to develop the Cornish Rex through breeding and Ms. Cox had seen a picture of one of their cats they had named Kallibunker.

She contacted the group about her cat and took Kirlee to be

bred with several of Kallibunker's descendants. However, despite several attempts at breeding Kirlee with the Cornish Rex cats, all of the kittens had straight fur coats.

Even though the two cat breeds were discovered geographically close to each other, it was determined that the gene that produced the curly fur of the Devon Rex was not the same one that produced curly fur in the Cornish Rex. The recessive genes were then named as (r) for the Cornish Rex and (re) for the Devon Rex.

In-breeding program

It was discovered that the only way to produce kittens with the curly fur was to in-breed the cat. Kirlee was carefully bred with the daughters produced from the Cornish-Devon Rex litters and the fur on the new kittens was curly.

The in-breeding program established the Devon Rex cat breed. The "Rex" in the name of these cats, as well as the Cornish Rex and the German Rex, refers to its fur. "Rexxed" means its fur is curly, which is why they are called Devon, for the city they were found in, and Rex, for their fur.

The Devon Rex is a small breed of cat, with most females weighing between four to six and a half pounds as adults and male adults will weigh between six and a half to nine pounds.

Chapter 1 - The Origins of the Devon Rex

Even though they look as if they could be frail cats, this breed is very muscular, agile and strong. They are very active and love to get into mischief, which is one of the reasons they are called "pixie" cats.

Genes and fur

Some of the kittens produced by this breed will have straight fur because it requires two of the recessive genes in the litter to have wavy furred cats. If only one of the genes is recessive for the fur, then the litter of kittens will be straight furred. However, the unique look that gives the Devon Rex the alternative nickname of "alien cat" is still present in all cats within the breed.

The curliness of the fur can vary among Devon Rex cats. Some of them will be born with a definite kink to their fur, while some of them will have a gentler wave, but all of their fur is very soft. Since it is so short, some people consider these cats hypoallergenic, although they are not officially a hypoallergenic breed since they do produce fur.

The patterns and colors of their fur vary greatly. You may have a Devon Rex that is solid colored or you may have one that has a tabby pattern to its coat. There are also tortoiseshell cats and those with points, not dissimilar to that of a Siamese. So, there is no standard color pattern to its fur that is associated with this cat breed. Therefore, all colors and patterns are considered for the breed in cat competitions.

As some pure bred animals can have health issues, in some countries, the Devon Rex has been cross-bred with Domestic cats to help increase the healthy gene pool for these cats. As a result, there are cats within the breed that have long, wavy fur.

As kittens, it can be difficult to tell the length of their fur because kittens will shed their fur, known as molting, at least once. However, if they were born with wavy or rippling fur, it will generally stay that way as adults.

Even though it had very humble beginnings, the Devon Rex is a prized cat breed that can now be found worldwide. These impish cats are not only loved for their unique look and soft, curly fur, but for their playful, mischievous personalities as well.

They make great family pets or these cats may be found on the floor of many cat shows around the world strutting their stuff.

Chapter 2 - Adopting a Devon Rex

As with most purebred cats, more than likely, you will never find a Devon Rex kitten at an ordinary pet shop or an animal shelter waiting to be adopted. If you do, you should snatch it up right away and take it home as a pet.

This breed was first imported to the United States from England in 1968, eight years after their first discovery, and they are now found anywhere in the world. The best place

Chapter 2 - Adopting a Devon Rex

to find Devon Rex kittens are in catteries that specialize in breeding this unique looking animal.

At home

If you want to add this cat to your family, you should do some research before you make a final decision. Where most cats are aloof, the Devon Rex is people oriented and they like a lot of attention.

They are very playful with plenty of energy to burn, so you have to be ready to entertain this cat by playing with him or her. At the very least, you need to be ready for it by buying it several toys so they can play and entertain themselves when no one is home.

A bored cat is often a curious cat and it might get into things that you don't want it to if you don't have enough toys to keep it occupied.

If you have other pets in the house, you don't have too much to worry about because the Devon Rex is a very sociable breed and they get along well with animals, they also do well with children.

Chapter 2 - Adopting a Devon Rex

How to locate a Devon Rex

The Internet is a good place to find catteries that specialize in the Devon Rex breed. The "Devon Rex Breed Club" is a great resource if you are interested in this cat and are thinking about adopting one for your home. The website for the DRBC can be found at

http://www.devonrexbreedclub.com/

Members of this club are breeders, owners and people who appreciate the breed. The DRBC provides all sorts of information about the Devon Rex, including information about rescuing older Devon Rex cats that need to find homes.

No matter where you live in the world, a good resource for finding a breeder is "Planet Devon" at

http://planetdevon.com/

They have a breeder's page in which you can locate a local breeder by using dropdown boxes to locate the country in which you live and narrow it down by the state, province or territory, depending on your country of origin. You can also search by the name of the cattery or breeder, if you know it.

Chapter 2 - Adopting a Devon Rex

Along with the breeder search page, Planet Devon also has a page dedicated to kittens and cats that are available for adoption. While most of the cats listed are Devon Rex there are others listed as well.

The search can be narrowed down by indicating whether you want a kitten or an adult by selecting the appropriate dropdown box. There are usually pictures and descriptions of the cats or kittens that are available for sale or for adoption.

Another good website to search for these cats is the "Fanciers Breeder Referral List," found at

http://www.breedlist.com/.

Although they are not exclusive to the Devon Rex breed, you can find information about where to find these cats by the location of catteries, you can search by breed, the name of the breeder, the name of the cattery or they list retired cats and news regarding kitten litters available for adoption.

It is rare to find a Devon Rex for adoption for free, so expect to pay for the cat or kitten and their shipping charges if you live in another state or country.

Chapter 2 - Adopting a Devon Rex

This site has a page for each breed that lists the standards and profiles from registries. They will have links to breeders' websites and breed club websites as well. Many of the club sites will list breeders, too. However, you must ask questions before you get a cat from a breeder to make sure you are buying one from a reputable breeder.

Questions to ask the breeder

Some of the questions you may want to ask or requests that you might wish to make when you are ready to adopt a cat or kitten are:

Ask if the kitten or cat's parents were certified. This helps you adopt a healthy cat because they have been certified "disease-free" from a veterinarian. Many breeds have diseases that offspring can inherit from their parents, including the Devon Rex. More will be covered about their health issues in a later chapter.

Try to meet the kittens' parents. This is a good way to check out the cats' temperament or evaluate them visually to see how healthy and well cared for that they look.

Ask if the kittens have been socialized.
Socialization is very important for kittens and needs to start at about six weeks of age to 16 weeks old. Socializing means having them handled by people, exposing them to other kittens other than their littermates and having them around cats of different ages. If the breeder has dogs, they may expose the kittens to them as well in order to teach them to get along with canines as well as other felines.

Ask about seeing the facility if you go pick out your Devon Rex kitten in person. A reputable breeder will have no problem with letting you inspect the home of the kitten you plan on adopting. If the breeder hedges or turns down your request, consider finding another breeder to deal with as one that doesn't allow you to see the facilities is probably hiding something.

Ask if the kitten has been updated on their shots, if they have been dewormed and about their visits to the veterinarian. Ask if the kitten has been declared healthy and if it hasn't, find out what problems he or she has. This will help you weed out sickly kittens, although it isn't an absolute guarantee that you will get a perfectly healthy kitten.

Find out if they have a guarantee on their kittens or cats. Ask what they do if you happen to adopt a kitten or cat with a serious illness or if it expires within weeks of its adoption. Purebred Devon Rex kittens are very expensive and you need to find out what happens if the kitten you adopt was sick.

Ask for referrals. Have the breeder refer to you some of their other customers and call them to find out about how their cat is and how they liked dealing with the breeder. If the breeder will not give you any referrals, they may have something to hide and you should consider trying another breeder.

With careful research and by asking questions, you can find a reputable breeder to buy a Devon Rex kitten from or you might want to consider getting a retired cat. A retired cat is one that was used for breeding and they have been retired by a breeder. If you don't have the time to put into a kitten, a retired cat is a great way to add a Devon Rex to your family.

Chapter 3 - Bringing Your New Kitten Home

When you do bring your new furry friend home, you need to know how to properly care for your Devon Rex kitten. Proper care for a kitten includes knowing how to properly groom their unique fur, what they should eat, and what shots they will need in the future.

When you purchase the kitten, you will want to make sure the breeder has kept up to date on their shots. This will help you know which shots they might need when you bring them home or which shots they will need in the future.

Kittens are usually weaned by the time they are eight weeks old, but most breeders will not adopt their kittens out until they are about four months old. By that time, the kitten should have most of their shots to protect them against rabies, feline leukemia, feline immunodeficiency virus and other disease that can attack kittens.

The last shots are administered at around 14 to 18 weeks of age and then usually require a yearly booster shot. The kitten should have been dewormed and treated for fleas as well.

What you need at first

The time to prepare to bring a new cat or kitten into your home is before you go pick him or her up. There are a number of supplies you will need to make the animal feel comfortable in their new home.

At the minimum, you will need a litter pan, a bed for him or her to sleep in, a water bowl, a food bowl and some toys. Of course, you will also need kitten food and litter for their toilet.

If possible, set up their supplies in an area that you can close off using a baby gate. Make sure the baby gate has small openings in it that your kitten cannot crawl through. The gate will help confine them to the areas they are allowed to roam, at least until they learn how to climb over it!

Chapter 3 - Bringing Your New Kitten Home

Using a baby gate to close them off into their area will allow your kitten to claim his or her territory and it will keep them confined to one area until they can get used to you and the rest of the family.

A baby gate will also allow them to look out and it will help them feel safe and secure by limiting them to their territory as well.

By being able to close them off from the rest of the house, at least until you've had them home for a few days, it will keep a small kitten from crawling behind a chair, sofa or into a cupboard and getting "lost" in your house.

Get them used to their new home

Even though your kitten has probably been socialized, they will need time to adjust to their new surroundings when you take them home. If they haven't been socialized well or if they are shy, they may immediately hide from you in their new home. Don't be surprised by this behavior and let them explore on their own so they are get familiar and acclimate to their new territory.

When you bring them home, be sure and introduce them to their toilet so they know where to use the restroom when they need to go. Ideally, this will be close to their area, but don't put it in the same vicinity near where you place their water and food.

No one, person nor animal, wants to eat near where they use the restroom. To help acquaint them to the house, you may want to feed them in the kitchen when it is breakfast and dinnertime.

Feeding Times

Just as you would for a human baby, you should keep your kitten on a feeding schedule. While many people like to free feed their cats, that means leaving a bowl of dry food out all day long, free feeding can lead to fat cats. It is better to have a set time of day that you feed your kitten so they get used to a feeding schedule.

A kitten less than six months old should be fed three times a day. Once they turn six months, you can cut that back to twice a day until they reach the age of nine months.

If you are not free feeding, keep them on a twice a day schedule so you can make sure they are eating enough food to stay healthy and to keep up with their energy needs. The Devon Rex cat is a high-energy cat, so they will need fuel to keep going all day long.

You can choose to feed your kitten dry cat foods made for their age group or you can feed them a raw diet. If you choose a raw diet, such as eggs, liver, chicken or other meats, you will need to give your kitten a calcium supplement until they are about nine months of age.

Dry foods, especially those for kittens, are supplemented with calcium, so they don't need any supplements. Once your kitten turns nine months old, you can start feeding him or her an adult diet.

Litter

When selecting litter for your kitten, don't use clumping litter when they're small. Curious kittens will sometimes eat the litter and, if it is a clumping litter, it could clump in their throats or stomach and kill the kitten.

Use a loose litter and make sure the litter box sides are short enough for the kitten to easily climb over. Keep the litter box very clean as well. If you notice the kitten is using the bathroom outside of the litter box that could indicate they either cannot climb into the litter box or that it isn't clean enough for them.

Cat trees

Invest in a cat tree and cat toys to keep them occupied when you have to go to work. Buy toys that you can use to play with them too, as they are social creatures and want to play with you as well as playing alone.

A cat tree allows them to climb, which all cats love to do, and they can also use it to sharpen their claws. If you don't get a cat tree, at least buy a scratching pad or post because it will help protect your furniture from their claws. Make sure you purchase one that uses sisal rope.

Many Devon Rex cats end up being lap kitties and they can be very vocal about their demands. While they can be independent, just as most cats can be, if you feel you don't have the time to devote to a kitten or a needy cat, don't select a Devon Rex.

They require a lot of attention from their owners, but you will be well rewarded with their affections if you do have the time to dote on them.

Chapter 4 - Properly Grooming Your Devon Rex

Making sure your cat is well groomed will not only keep them looking beautiful, but it will help keep them healthy as well. Grooming not only means paying attention to their fur, but making sure their nails are trimmed, their eyes are clean, their teeth clean and keeping their skin clean as well.

Their fur

The Devon Rex is a low maintenance cat as their fur is very

short, but it is delicate, so you need to take care when you brush or comb them.

The fur of a Devon Rex may be either gently wavy or it may have tight curls, although their curls not as tight as their cousin's fur, the Cornish Rex. Usually kittens that have curly or wavy fur will have that same fur as adults, but kittens do shed, or molt, their fur at least once when they are young.

The fur on their sides, back, tail, legs, face and ears is usually the thickest, while the fur on their head, neck, chest and belly is the thinnest. However, they should never have bald spots.

When you need or want to brush or comb their fur, do so gently. It is delicate and, if you groom them roughly, their fur can be damaged. Their skin may sometimes have a greasy feel to it, especially in the folds of their skin or around the paws.

If this happens, you just need to bathe them every few weeks. If you start when they are young, you can get them used to bathing in water or you can use a dry shampoo on your cat.

Since their fur is short, they don't require a lot of grooming to keep it looking clean and neat. However, it is important to get your cat used to being groomed, so you will want to gently brush or comb their fur and handle their paws frequently.

Teaching them how to be handled when they are groomed will keep them from scratching or biting you during the process.

Along with caring for their beautiful fur and skin, you will need to keep your Devon Rex's nails trimmed as well. Their nails grow faster than most other breeds, so make sure they are trimmed often, sometimes as often as once a week.

Nails

Their claws are clear, so it is easy to see the quick, which you need to avoid when clipping a cat's nails.

The nails don't have nerves, so they don't hurt when they are trimmed. The quick does have nerves and, if it is accidentally clipped, not only will it be painful for your cat, but it will bleed as well. Be careful when clipping their nails so you can avoid clipping the quick.

When you are ready to clip the cat's nails you'll need a pet nail clipper. They are only a few dollars from a local pet store and are specially designed for pets. I would not recommend a human nail clipper.

Just put the paw in your hand and gently press down on it with your thumb. The cat's claws will extend and you can start clipping them.

Don't clip them too much usually just the sharp point or the hook of the claw will be sufficient. A scratch pad or post is essential because this will help keep their claws shortened and sharp.

Teeth care

Tooth decay and gum disease are problems for many cats, but you can head off some of these issues by learning to brush your cat's teeth. If you start training them as kittens, you can get them used to having their teeth brushed and prevent problems for them later in life.

Not only can plaque accumulate on their teeth from food and bacteria, but also bacteria can sometimes get into their bloodstream and damage their internal organs.

It isn't uncommon for older cats to lose teeth to these problems and learning to brush their teeth will help the cat keep them longer. Your veterinarian can show you how to brush your kitten's teeth and advise you on the type of brush to use, as well as the type of dental products you may need.

Plaque usually builds up on the outside, not the inside, of their teeth, so it isn't all that hard to learn how to brush them, it just takes time and patience.

If you have young kittens, don't brush their milk teeth as they will fall out and be replaced by permanent teeth, but it is a good time to start getting them used to having their teeth touched.

Gently open their lips and touch their teeth with your finger, so they will get used to it. This will help make them easier to train when it comes time to actually brush their teeth.

Sometimes cats will not tolerate having their teeth brushed no matter what you do. If this is the case, have your veterinarian recommend an oral product to give them to keep their teeth healthy. Along with brushing their teeth, you can feed your adult cat dental formula dry food. This type of food helps keep a cat's teeth cleaner and healthier.

Chapter 4 - Properly Grooming Your Devon Rex

Eye care

Eye care is an important part of your cat's grooming routine as well. Some cats get "sleep" in their eyes that may need to be gently wiped away.

You can use a cotton swab to gently wipe their eye from the nose side outwards and use a clean swab for each eye. If they get discharge in their eye, wipe it away using the same method and contact your vet if it lasts for more than two days.

Having a regular grooming routine will help keep your Devon Rex cat healthy, happy and looking beautiful. Start working on their beauty routine as soon as you bring them home to help them get used to being brushed and handled. The less stressful it is on them, the better for both of you.

Chapter 5 - Health Issues Found in the Devon Rex Breed

It isn't uncommon for some purebred pets to have medical issues, especially a breed like the Devon Rex that has been inbred. The Devon Rex has its share of inherited diseases that they need to be checked for in order to make sure they are healthy or if they are carriers of a disease.

Chapter 5 - Health Issues Found in the Devon Rex Breed

There are a few diseases this breed is known to carry genes for that can be passed on to the offspring including: pseudohemophilia, patella luxation, and hereditary myopathy.

Pseudohemophilia,

which is also known as Von Willebrand Disease, is a blood disorder that is most common in humans and dogs. It is rarely found in cats, but it is a genetic disorder found in the Devon Rex breed.

This disorder doesn't allow the blood to clot normally, which can lead to excessive blood loss if they are injured or undergo surgery. The blood loss can lead to anemia or it can be life threatening.

There is no known cure for pseudohemophilia at this time, so it is important to take precautions if you find out your cat has this condition. The signs of the disorder in your cat could be bleeding from the gums, nosebleeds and excessive bruising.

A blood test can help determine if your cat has this disorder. It is important to note that all Devon Rex cats have type B blood and transfusing them with another blood type can be fatal.

Chapter 5 - Health Issues Found in the Devon Rex Breed

Hypertrophic cardiomyopathy,

HCM, is one of the most common forms of heart disease in cats. The disease causes the heart muscle to thicken, which keeps the heart from beating normally. It is usually fatal in cats and it doesn't only affect the Devon Rex, but it is found in all breeds. HCM is detected by doing an echocardiogram.

When you are looking to adopt a Devon Rex kitten, avoid breeders claiming to produce HCM-free lines as no one can guarantee that a cat will not have HCM.

All Devon Rex cats should be screened for the disease, especially if they are going to be bred. If HCM is detected, that cat should not be used for breeding as the disease is hereditary and they can pass it on to their offspring.

Patella luxation

Another hereditary issue that the Devon Rex can pass on to his or her offspring is patella luxation. The patella is the kneecap and, in a Devon Rex with this problem, it occasionally pops out of place.

If you notice your cat hopping or limping, it may have this problem. Usually, the patella may pop back into place on its own, but, if your cat has a severe case, the dislocated may occur frequently or be permanent. In severe cases, surgical correction will probably be needed.

When you do adopt a Devon Rex kitten, ask the breeder to show that the kitten has been screened for these two problems. If they cannot produce documentation that shows the kitten hasn't been screened for these hereditary conditions, find another breeder.

They should be able to easily produce any paperwork needed to show that their cats and kittens have been screened for diseases.

Hip dysplasia

Hip dysplasia can also occur in this breed, but it is a problem that can occur in any mammal that has hips, including humans.

The socket of the hip joint may be shallow, which causes it to wear with use as the ball of the joint rubs against the socket, causing hip dysplasia. It can be hard to detect in cats because they are so lightweight that many cases go undetected.

If you notice your cat walking gingerly, with an odd gait or if your cat seems to be in pain when you touch the hip area, you should take him or her to your veterinarian for an examination.

The hip can be dislocated if they have an advanced case of this joint problem. Hip dysplasia is detected by an x-ray and it may require surgical correction, including a hip replacement, if the case is severe.

Cats should be routinely vaccinated against:

- Feline infectious enteritis
- Feline herpes virus
- Feline calicivirus
- Feline leukaemia virus*.

*Current recommendations are that only at risk cats are given vaccine against feline leukemia virus.

Overall Health

Despite these issues, the Devon Rex is a relatively healthy breed. Some breeders have made an effort to breed them with other cats, especially domestic cats, to make them healthier and to try to breed out health issues, such as pseudohemophilia.

When you do adopt a Devon Rex, make sure the breeder has a medical clearance for the cat you adopt and ask about their guarantee if a series illness is detected.

Chapter 5 - Health Issues Found in the Devon Rex Breed

The best way to keep your cat healthy is to feed him or her a healthy diet so they maintain their proper weight. This will keep pressure off their joints, which means they won't wear down as fast as they would in a heavier cat. Along with the proper diet, keep them active and take them to the vet for regular check-ups to make sure they are healthy.

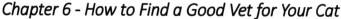

Chapter 6 - How to Find a Good Vet for Your Cat

To make sure your cat stays happy and healthy, you need to find a veterinarian you can trust to treat him or her. The time to look for a veterinarian isn't during an emergency, but before you bring your new family member home.

A good way to find a vet is to ask the pet lovers in your life who they take their pets to and ask how they like that veterinarian. You will quickly learn who to consider and who to eliminate from your search for a vet.

In many larger communities, you will be able to find veterinarians that specialize in cat care. Although you don't necessarily need to choose a vet that specializes in cats, it may be better since you own one that is purebred.

The specialists have been trained how to handle cats and educated in diseases that affect cats. In some areas, you may not have a cat-only veterinarian available, but if you do, consider taking your cat to a doctor that has specialized in treating them.

The veterinarian is only one part of the team that will treat your cat. There are also technicians, assistants and other support staff that may help care for your pet. You should evaluate their ability to handle your cat in a caring, competent manner as well.

Also, check the fees and how far from your home that you have to take your cat if you have an emergency. Driving a few extra miles or paying a bit more for good care may be well worth the effort for your Devon Rex.

Go online to check for the nearest cat hospitals and veterinarians in your area. Most businesses have websites and you will be able to get information on their hours, the services they offer for your cat and they may even include information about their staff. The Internet is a good resource to use when looking for a doctor for your pet, as well as other information about the Devon Rex breed.

Chapter 6 - How to Find a Good Vet for Your Cat

Check the veterinarians that you find online or those who have been recommended to you for accreditation from the American Animal Hospital Association. The accreditation process for the AAHA is voluntary and it shows that the facility has met the association's standards for quality care, equipment and for the facility itself.

If you ever need a specialist to treat your cat, ask if they have board certification. That requires an additional two to four years of study in the area of their specialty and then they have to pass the rigorous exam that is required to receive their certification. If the vet specialist is not board certified, pass on him or her and find one that is, if it is possible where you live.

After you've decided on a few veterinarians from your area, you need to schedule a time to go meet them and tour their facility. Not only does a good vet need to have great rapport with animals, but they should have good rapport with their owners as well.

Go and meet them before you need to

Take the time to meet the staff, try to observe how they interact with pets and their owners, as well as check out the facility as your tour it. Most vets will be happy to let you tour their facility and you should be wary of those who refuse your request.

Chapter 6 - How to Find a Good Vet for Your Cat

Before going to your appointment, write down any questions that you may have for the vet, especially asking about their experience with the Devon Rex breed. If they do have experience treating Devon Rexes, then that is a big plus for them.

Questions to ask

Ask questions to learn about the policies of the facility and find out their philosophy about treating pets.

There is a lot you can learn by observing the veterinarian's office as you tour the facilities. You can check to make sure that the facility is kept clean, organized and if it looks comfortable for the pets being treated.

If the facility treats both dogs and cats, check to see if the cages are kept in separate areas or if they are put in the same room. If you see something you don't like, don't be afraid to question it.

Find out if EKGs, x-rays, ultrasound and other testing is done in-house or if you would have to visit a specialist to get the tests done. Check to see if they have in-house lab facilities to analyze blood work or if that is sent to an outside lab. If they do send it to a lab that may mean it will be longer for you to get information on lab results and that can be vital if your cat is seriously ill.

Also, ask about their availability for emergency treatment and ask which services they offer for emergencies. Find out about any costs that will be involved when bringing your pet in for check-ups or treatment and ask about senior discounts, if applicable, or multi-pet discounts.

Budget shouldn't be your first consideration when selecting a vet, but for some people, it can be important information to know.

Once you've selected a veterinarian for your new cat, you need to develop a good rapport with them. You need to play your part in the relationship by bringing in your Devon Rex for their check-ups and not just when they are sick.

This will help the vet to get to know both you and your cat, which will help them whenever they need to treat your cat.

Observe your cat so that you know what their normal behavior is, which will make it easier for you to determine when they are not feeling well. Don't wait until the cat has gotten worse to call your vet.

Chapter 6 - How to Find a Good Vet for Your Cat

Often times your pet will have something that can be treated if you take them in right away. If you wait, your vet may not be able to treat your cat successfully. In many cases, time is of the essence when your cat has taken ill and it is important you have them treated right away.

Whenever you do take your cat to see the vet, take him or her in a cat carrier to make it more comfortable for everyone involved. Many cats do not like taking car rides and having a good cat carrier will be the only way you will be able to travel with them, whether it is just across town or longer distances.

To get them used to traveling in a carrier, use it when you first bring them home so they know what to expect from a young age.

Between the times you pick out your Devon Rex kitty until the time the breeder released him or her into your care, you should have plenty of opportunity to pick out a vet. Developing a relationship with them by taking your cat in for shots and regular check-ups, plus being a responsible owner when you are at their office, will go a long way into developing a lasting rapport with your cat's chosen veterinarian.

Chapter 7 - The Playful Personality of the Devon Rex

This impish looking little cat maybe small in stature, but they have a huge personality that people love. They are

Chapter 7 - The Playful Personality of the Devon Rex

playful, mischievous, energetic and, unlike most cats, they are seldom aloof.

Devon Rex characteristics

While there are times when they show their independent streaks, for the most part, the Devon Rex is a very social cat. They like being around their owners, the other cats in the family and they will even tolerant the presence of a dog, if they must.

The Devon Rex are a smart breed and they are very inquisitive, which means you need to keep track of what you leave out when they are roaming the house. They may try sampling the houseplants that you have, which can make them ill, as many houseplants are poisonous for cats. However, that also means they easily learn tricks if you are willing to take the time to train them.

This breed has been playfully referred to as the "poodle of the cat world" because of their rexxed fur and their almost dog-like qualities of loyalty and love for their human owners. These cats likes to eat, sleep and follow their humans around their houses as they wait for the chance to curl up in laps or sit at your feet. Even if you are just doing chores, the Devon Rex will follow you around, trying to "help" by cooing and trilling as you try to work.

Chapter 7 - The Playful Personality of the Devon Rex

These cats, unlike many of their independent minded cousins, are very social and they don't do well without companionship for very long.

Children are perfect companions for these highly energetic cats as they love to play and cuddle with their human companions. However, a Devon Rex is not discriminatory and will generally get along with humans, other cats, dogs and even the odd rabbit or bird alike.

If you are out of the house for most of the day, your Devon can keep itself occupied and generally stay out of mischief.

Be careful with food around your Devon Rex because he or she will try being clever, as well as adorable, while trying to snatch food off your plate. As with their companions, they also don't discriminate when it comes to food.

No matter what you have on your plate, they will try to sample some of it. Keep them on their feeding schedule no matter how much they try to cajole you into thinking they are starving. As long as they are being fed at their regular times, they are not hungry, they are just expressing their love for food.

If they do manage to get you to share some of your food with them, be careful about what your cat is allowed to eat. While a small bit of meat may be okay on occasion, avoid giving them anything with onions, grapes, raisins, garlic, chocolate or avocado in it. These substances contain toxins that can make your cat very ill. Also, don't feed them cow's milk because it will give them diarrhea.

Personality

The Devon Rex breed has a great personality and an even temperament, which makes them a great family pet. When they do talk, their voices are quiet, so don't expect a lot of feedback when they are around you. Aside from cooing or trilling, they often don't have much to say, but they are ready to play when you are and vie for your affections whenever they can.

Since they are a high-energy cat, they need plenty of toys to keep themselves occupied and for you to play with them as well. A cat tree would be a good investment, because otherwise these spunky creatures may take to climbing your drapes as they play around the house. Keep a good supply of soft toys around the house that your cat can bat around or carry to entertain themselves while you're out for the day. Invest in cat wand toys so you can play with them, too.

Just as you might for a human child, try to keep chemicals and substances toxic to cats out of reach, even if you have to use baby proofing hardware to lock your cabinet doors.

Chapter 7 - The Playful Personality of the Devon Rex

Once they have full reign of your house, they will investigate it thoroughly and they could accidentally poison themselves if you are not careful about keeping things away from them. They love to jump, so even if you put these items on high shelves, they can still get to them.

If you are looking for an affectionate, playful clown of a cat that doesn't go out of its way to avoid all human contact, the Devon Rex is the perfect choice.

Given the chance it will shower you with love, cuddle on your lap, snuggle in bed with you and follow you everywhere around your house. Be prepared to play at a moment's notice or have an armful of cat because the Devon Rex is the perfect companion cat.

Chapter 8 - Cat Misbehaviors and Causes

Even the mildest mannered cat can have behavior problems, but by eliminating any possible physical problems causing the bad behavior and retraining your cat, you can easily overcome these issues.

While the Devon Rex breed is known for its playful, loving personality, some of these cats can still have issues, especially if they had a rough beginning in life. Some behavior problems may be a sign that your cat is getting older, it could be because of a dietary deficiency or bad behaviors may come from just being bored.

Some behavior problems you may notice from your cat could be: not using the litter box when they soil, chewing or scratching destructively, excessive meowing or aggressive behavior toward humans and/or other pets.

Although you may consider it bad behavior, sometimes there are physical reasons why your cat starts behaving in this manner and it is important to recognize the change in their personality so you are able to tell when something is wrong with them.

Problems?

There are many behavior issues that a cat can develop as it gets older. The cat may have a physical ailment or an older adopted cat may have issues if it had a traumatic background. Here are some of the cat behavior issues that you should know about.

Excessive Vocalization

Although a Devon Rex will playfully seek your attention or, sometimes, just jump onto your shoulder or lap to get attention, excessive attention seeking can annoy some people.

Chapter 8 - Cat Misbehaviors and Causes

A common complaint about cat behavior is loud crying or meowing. As a Devon has an usually quiet voice, this should be cause for concern if they suddenly start loudly meowing or yowling.

Causes for excessive vocalization can be either physical or emotional, although for some cats it can be normal behavior. It is possible to have a Devon who likes to talk, although they usually do so more quietly than other breeds of cats.

As your cat ages, they may tend to "howl" at night, sounding as if they are lost. The causes for this behavior can be deafness in a cat or senility, as they get older.

Avoiding the litter box

Soiling in the house is the number one reason cats are often surrendered to animal shelters, but it can also be easily remedied in many cases. If your cat suddenly starts eliminating outside of the litter box, the first step you should take is to clean it more frequently.

Most cats will not use a dirty litter box and they may take to eliminating nearby it. If the litter box is in the bathroom, they may start eliminating in your bathtub or on the floor near the litter box.

Chapter 8 - Cat Misbehaviors and Causes

Another cause for this could be physical. If your cat has a urinary tract infection, it may not be able to make it to the box on time. If they have hemorrhoids or if they are constipated, they will sometimes potty outside of their litter box.

If the litter box is clean and these issues still exist, make an appointment with your veterinarian and have your cat checked for physical causes that lead to eliminating outside of the litter box.

Spraying Urine

Cats will often spray urine to mark their territory outside, but if they start doing it inside, it could be either marking territory or it could be a sign of stress. Since cats are creatures of habit, they may not respond well to changes in their cat universe.

Changes that may stress your cat could be the addition of a new pet into the household, the addition of a baby, moving to another home, an illness or death of a pet or human family member.

If you have had changes in your household and your cat does start spraying, try to reassure him or her with some extra attention. Once they know everything is okay, they should stop that behavior.

However, it is important to eliminate the odor by using an enzymatic product, which neutralizes the bacteria causing the odor. If the scent isn't eliminated, your cat will return and keep spraying in the same place.

Destructive Chewing

This should be a cause for concern because some of the items your cat may choose to chew on could be harmful to them or they could be valuable to you. There can be many causes for destructive chewing, including teething in kittens, boredom or, especially in the case of the Devon Rex, curiosity.

Excessive chewing can also be caused by a deficiency in their diet as well.

Make sure you are feeding them a healthy, well-balanced diet so they remain healthy and active. For teething, try giving your kitten large straws to chew on and play with or you can get them soft toys they can chew on as well.

Discourage chewing on cords, which can be tempting for playful cats, and houseplants by making them taste bad with apple bitter or a gentle spray from a water bottle if you catch them chewing on something they shouldn't.

Chapter 8 - Cat Misbehaviors and Causes

Destructive Scratching

Even if your cat has a cat tree or plenty of scratching posts to scratch on, they may still scratch your furniture or your carpet. Scratching is exercise for your cat, it works as a stress reliever and it helps keep their claws well maintained.

Make sure that you have plenty of scratching surfaces available to your cat to keep them away from furniture and carpets.

If they do start scratching on furniture or carpets, discourage it by a short burst of water from a spray bottle, trim their claws, or if the situation is bad enough, use nail caps. Do not resort to declawing your cat because that is like cutting off their fingers. A cat uses its claws to grip when they climb and pull things to themselves. Declawing should never be a consideration.

Along with these physical manifestations of cat misbehavior, cats can also have anxiety, depression or other psychological issues that causes "misbehavior." Cat psychology problems will be covered in the next chapter.

Always try to eliminate any physical causes of your cat's behavior before trying other options. If your Devon Rex starts behaving oddly, schedule an appointment with your veterinarian for a check-up. Catching an ailment quickly will allow your cat to be treated and fully recover from any health problems they might be experiencing.

Chapter 9 - Kitty Psychology: Dealing with Shyness or Fear

Cats can also suffer from behavioral issues stemming from stress, anxiety, depression and they can display OCD behaviors as well. It is very important to know how your cat normally acts and behaves so you can spot problems quickly.

Chapter 9 - Kitty Psychology: Dealing with Shyness or Fear

If you know what to look for, you can help your cat by soothing them or getting them treated by your veterinarian as "bad" behaviors by cats often have a physical cause, such as an illness. The quicker the problem is found, the more likely it can be treated successfully.

Although the Devon Rex breed is not known for their shyness, not every cat is going to have the same personality as their ancestors. It isn't uncommon for some cats to be shy or skittish, especially when they are in a new environment.

That is one reason you will want to put your new cat into an area that you can close off with a baby gate. It will give them time to acclimate to their new surroundings, but you will want to interact with them as well to help make their transition to their new home a smooth one.

Shyness

Sometimes it isn't shyness that the cat is displaying, but fear. Fear and shyness can have the same root causes, but with patience, you can help them overcome their fear. You need to let the cat set his or her own pace; otherwise they may feel cornered and resort to fighting you or the other animals they are around.

Shyness or fear isn't necessarily a personality trait that your cat is stuck with because there are sometimes unresolved medical issues that can cause their shyness.

Whenever you bring a new cat into your household, regardless if you just bought it from breeder or adopted it from a shelter, you should make an appointment with your veterinarian to have him or her examined.

Causes

Any underlying medical issues that the cat may have can then be detected and resolved. Even though you may have papers that say your Devon Rex has a clean bill of health, a check-up by your vet should still be performed.

Another underlying cause of shyness or fear in a cat may stem from poor socialization. A kitten's mother usually socializes the kitten with other cats, animals and humans, but if the kitten was removed from her care at a young age, he or she may have not been properly socialized.

A kitten should stay with its mother for at least the first eight weeks of its life, although 12 weeks is optimal and they are usually fully socialized by that time.

Changes in environment, such as moving into a new home, can cause your cat to be scared or shy as well. Even humans get shy when they are introduced into a new environment, such as a new school or new job, so it stands to reason that a cat moving into a home they are unfamiliar with may experience shyness or fear as well.

Patience is the key to helping your new cat deal with its shyness. Gently pet him or her while speaking in a soft voice to try to reassure your cat. Let them explore their surroundings on their own and they will quickly get used to their new home on their own terms.

However, for cats that are shy or fearful, don't be surprised if they hide away for a few days, sometimes as much as two weeks. Make sure fresh water and a fresh litter box are always accessible to them, stick to a feeding schedule and leave out toys for them. As they get comfortable, they will emerge and start making themselves at home.

Aggression

Many of the same reasons that cause shyness will also cause your cat to be fearful and, sometimes, a fearful cat can be an aggressive cat.

When you are dealing with a cat that seems to be afraid of you, don't stare at him directly in the eyes. For cats, this is a sign of aggression that will trigger a "flight" or "fight" response. Most likely, the cat will want to flee, unless it feels trapped and then it may come out swinging.

Chapter 9 - Kitty Psychology: Dealing with Shyness or Fear

If you have other cats, you need to gradually introduce a new one into your home, which is another reason a baby gate is a good investment. The gate allows you to close off the new cat into its area and keeps your other cats, or dogs, at bay. However, they can still see each other through the gate and get acquainted with each other without being able to attack.

Loud noises and environment disasters can be a source of fear for cats. While the loud noises can be easily dealt with, the unexpected disaster isn't as easy. For the most part, you know if there is construction scheduled for your neighborhood or you know on New Year's Eve and the Fourth of July there are going to be fireworks.

If your cat is bothered by loud noises, put your cat in a place where they feel safe so they won't be as frightened by the loud sounds.

If you live in an area where there are tornadoes, hurricanes or where other disasters occur, be prepared with an evacuation kit for your pets.

For your Devon Rex, this will include a cat carrier, food, some water, a litter box and litter, a toy or two and something you can give them for stress. It will be far easier to deal with their fears if you are prepared and, once everyone is back home, you can begin to soothe your cat's

Chapter 9 - Kitty Psychology: Dealing with Shyness or Fear

anxiety.

Fear and shyness are not the only psychological issues that can occur in cats. They may also deal with depression, OCD behaviors and stress.

However, shyness and fear are going to be the most common behaviors you will find in cats, even for cats with a pleasant temperament. If you are patient with them and show them love, they will usually recover from their fears or shyness.

Chapter 10 - Kitty Psychology: Odd Cat Behaviors

Even the most normal seeming cats will behave oddly sometimes and it is important to be able to interpret their behavior to understand why they are behaving in an odd manner.

Some issues can be psychological, such as OCD behaviors, and some of their antics are playful. If you understand their behaviors, you will enjoy your cat even more and realize when you need to get them help.

Chapter 10 - Kitty Psychology: Odd Cat Behaviors

After reading the previous chapter, you should be able to spot the signs of shyness or fear in your cat and begin to understand why they may be showing signs of stress or anxiety.

Not only should you have a better understanding of those behaviors, but you also can start helping to alleviate your cat's fears and shyness with patience, understanding and love.

Some of the behaviors stemming from stress may include grooming too much or excessive licking. If you've spent any time with cats, then you know they will groom themselves when they are anxious or if they've committed a blunder, such as falling off a piece of furniture.

Over-grooming

While there are some medical causes for over-grooming that you should investigate including fleas, allergies and fungal infections, there are reasons that are more psychological as well.

Over-grooming may be a symptom of psychogenic alopecia, which can cause your cat to lick or groom themselves to the point they are balding in some areas. If there is no underlying medical cause for their behavior, over-grooming is a sign of stress.

Chapter 10 - Kitty Psychology: Odd Cat Behaviors

The act of licking or grooming themselves is a soothing behavior for cats and researchers claim that it helps release endorphins in the brain, which give a cat pleasure and act as a pain reliever.

Your veterinarian needs to diagnose the condition, but if your cat licks itself excessively, make an appointment to take him or her in for a check-up. There are some things you can do to help reduce your cat's stress, including cuddling and playtime, but your vet may put the cat on an anti-anxiety medication if the problem cannot be resolved by any other means.

Sucking and chewing

Another OCD behavior some cats will exhibit is wool sucking or chewing. This behavior is caused when a cat has been taken away from its mother at an early age.

When they need comfort, they will knead a blanket and suck or chew on it, much they did as a kitten feeding from its mother's teat. That was their first experience with comfort and, if they haven't been socialized properly, they will resort back to it, even as a grown cat.

A cat that does this may also suck on your finger, themselves or another cat seeking this comfort. Wool sucking isn't a cause for concern and it can be a good bonding experience to have with a cat who exhibits the behavior.

Just be sure they are not ingesting the material they are sucking on and help comfort them as they suck by gently stroking them and using a calm soothing voice when speaking to them.

Some of your cat's behaviors will be more playful and fun as they try to communicate with you in any way they can. Some of their antics may include:

Rolling on the Ground –

If you've ever seen a cat suddenly flop to the ground before you and roll over onto its back, it is merely trying to get your attention. They will usually rub their head or back against the floor as they flop at your feet and wait for you to pet them.

However, don't assume your cat wants you to rub its stomach. If you do, they may grab your hand, nip and kick at it.

Chapter 10 - Kitty Psychology: Odd Cat Behaviors

A cat on its back is actually in a defensive posture. Being on their back allows them to use all of their claws and teeth together in order to defend themselves. When you rub its belly, your cat interprets the action as an attack and it will grab your hand, scratch, bite or use its back paws to kick you.

Bunting –

If you're ever had a cat head-bottom or body bump you, they are leaving their scent on you and offering a sign of trust with this attention. The official term for this behavior is bunting or allorubbing. Cats have scent glands all over their bodies, including around their chin, ears, the corners of their mouth, their temples and tail.

Sometimes your cat may head-bottom you similar to how goats will bump heads and other times they will rub their head against your head, your hands or rub their body against you.

Basically, they are rubbing their scent on you. However, if they do head-bottom you while their eyes are open, they are showing you a sign of trust as they only perform this behavior with other cats that are friendly.

Chapter 10 - Kitty Psychology: Odd Cat Behaviors

Bottom Presentation - Do you find it odd that your cat likes to show off their bottom to you? Well, it isn't meant to be offensive and it is actually a compliment. By showing you their bottom, your cat is giving you an enthusiastic greeting. They will do this with other cats that they know well and that they trust.

Cats often smell each other in greeting, first around the head and neck, then along the flanks. Finally, they will greet each other with a sniff on the rear. If their tail is raised, the cat is signifying that it isn't a threat to their other feline friends.

Cat Blinks - Sometimes your cat looks like he is winking or flirting with you by half-closing his eyes and he may well be. The eye blink is a cat's version of a kiss. They will do this with other friendly cats and with the people they love. Cats use their eyes to communicate their intentions to other cats and even to humans.

If they stare at another cat, they are attempting to intimidate them, as it is an aggressive posture, but the cat blink or kiss is a non-threatening gesture and it shows their good intentions.

They will usually repeat it when it is done to them, so the next time you have your cat's attention, try giving them a slow blink and you will probably get a kiss in return.

Chapter 10 - Kitty Psychology: Odd Cat Behaviors

Phones and Cats - Cats, like the Devon Rex, are very inquisitive, so when they hear a noise, they are likely to go investigate it. When your phone rings, it probably triggers your cat's curiosity and they will come over to you to find out what is going on.

When they hear you talking, but they don't see whom you are talking to, they may assume you are speaking with them. If they do, more vocal cats may start to answer you by meowing. Don't be annoyed if they seem fascinated when you are on the phone, they are just being their curious selves.

Cats have many other behaviors that you can learn. Their seemingly odd antics are often not so odd at all and it could be their way of trying to communicate with you. Learn these behaviors so you know how to "talk" to your cat, too.

Chapter 11 - Are You Ready to Adopt a Cat?

Although most cats are very independent, you are a very necessary component to their care. While they may seem as if they don't need you at times, the

Chapter 11 - Are You Ready to Adopt a Cat?

Devon Rex is a very social oriented breed and they crave your attention.

They need you to play, cuddle and care for them, but sometimes owners get negligent when it comes to taking care of cats because they assume cats don't need as much care as a dog might.

Before you adopt any cat, especially a social cat like the Devon Rex, you need to determine if you have the time to invest in cat care. While a kitten is cute and cuddly, if you don't have time to devote to him or her, you shouldn't adopt one.

It doesn't require a large invest of time to properly care for a cat, but with a Devon, you will need to put up with crawling into your bed, onto your lap and play with him or her to burn off some of their energy.

Too many people adopt cats on the spur of the moment without thinking the decision through and then, when they do something they feel is intolerable, instead of taking time to figure out what the problem is, they surrender them to a shelter.

By researching and doing your homework, you can make an informed decision about whether you have the time and resources to adopt a cat, especially one that does need your attention like a Devon Rex.

Costs

It is also necessary to determine if you can financially afford to adopt a purebred cat like a Devon. Not only are you going to pay much more than you would to adopt a Domestic breed, but you will also have additional costs associated with caring for your cat.

Adopting a Devon Rex can cost anywhere from $300 to $1,000, depending on the breeder and the age of the cat.

With most breeders, you will pay more for a kitten than you will for an adult cat. Most of the adult cats available for adoption have been retired from breeding and breeders want to find them a forever home after they are no longer producing kittens. Even though an adult Devon will still want your attention, they don't require as much care as an inquisitive kitten and they make better pets for busy people.

Along with the costs associated with adopting your cat, you will also need to buy supplies for it, such as

Chapter 11 - Are You Ready to Adopt a Cat?

a litter box, litter, food, toys, scratching posts, and a cat bed if you don't want it to sleep with you.

It is also necessary to keep up with your cat's medical check-ups and shots in order to keep him or her healthy. It is far less expensive, monetarily and emotionally, to maintain your cat's healthy that it is to have a sick feline friend that requires emergency care.

You can easily spend about $50 to $60 per month just keep up with your cat's basic necessities, never mind any extras that you may wish to buy them.

It is a good idea to have a savings account dedicated to your pet in case you need to take them to an emergency vet or for other unexpected medical expenses that can come up. Try saving at least $10 to $20 per month for your cat so you can afford trips for future emergency care.

Unless you plan to breed your Devon Rex, to help maintain his or her health, you should spay or neuter your cat. In male cats, it can help prevent behavior problems if he is neutered.

If he hasn't been neutered, he is more like to spray urine, he may be more aggressive with other cats, he will want to try to escape to find a female to mate with, and he is at greater risk for testicular and mammary cancers.

Unspayed female cats of course are at risk for becoming pregnant if they get out of your house, but they also spray to attract males and they are at greater risks for uterine, ovarian and mammary cancers.

They can also develop pyometritis, which infects the uterus of cats about a week after they have gone into heat. It is a potentially fatal disease that can be prevented if you spay your female cat.

Inside / Outside

Even if you have a fenced backyard, try not to let your cats roam free outside. Devons love to climb and jump, so a tree or a fence will not deter them from getting out of your yard. If they are outside, they can be subject to fights with stray cats, attacks from stray dogs, bit by insects or, if they wander out into the street, they can be accidentally run over and killed by a car.

A neutered or spayed cat will be less likely to want to go outside, so that is another advantage to making

Chapter 11 - Are You Ready to Adopt a Cat?

sure your cat is spayed or neutered.

If your cat wants to be outside, create an outdoor fenced in cat area where they can be safe, but still enjoy the feel of grass under their paws, fresh air and sunshine.

If you have a patio, consider fencing it in with chicken wire so they can't get out and put a cat tree in it so they can have a place to lie down and observe Mother Nature. A mesh gazebo that people use for picnics outdoors is a good option as well. However, keeping them indoors is preferable.

Many inexperienced cat owners assume that cats can care for their own grooming needs because they give themselves baths, but they need your help there as well. Your Devon Rex will need your help with the occasional gentle brushing and, since their claws grow faster than most other breeds, you will need to keep their claws clipped by maintaining about once a week.

Occasionally, you may need to give your cat a bath. They are curious creatures and they may sometimes make messes, get dirty and need to be bathed. Fortunately, a Devon Rex is a wash-n-go cat, so you can bathe them and leave them to their own devices afterwards.

Care

Although, during the winter months, you may want to wrap them in a warm, fluffy towel to dry before letting them loose in the house. Contrary to popular belief, most cats are not afraid of water and if you start bathing them at a young age, they will get used to water baths.

Dental care is very important for cats and you will need to be proactive to help them keep their teeth clean and healthy. Plaque build-up can cause bacteria to rot their teeth, give them gingivitis and the bacteria can even get into their bloodstream. Bacteria in their blood can damage their internal organs, which can be fatal.

If you start taking care of your cat's teeth when they are young, they will let you gently brush their teeth to keep them healthy and plaque free. Brushing helps your cat keep their teeth as they get older and reduces bad breath. There are dental products made especially for cats that your veterinarian can advise you on.

Adopting and caring for a cat is a lot of

Chapter 11 - Are You Ready to Adopt a Cat?

responsibility, but if you have the time and are financially able to properly care for a Devon Rex, you will be rewarded many times over by their affections and love. The bond between a cat and its human can be special and it is well worth the effort that is required from you.

Chapter 12 - Clicker Training for Your Cat

Although many people think of cats as stubborn and too independent to learn, their behaviors can be corrected and they are capable of learning tricks. Whether you are trying to redirect your cat's behavior or trying to teach it a trick, your Devon Rex wants to please you and it can be easily trained. One of the best methods to use when trying to correct behaviors is to employ clicker training.

Clicker training, which is officially called operant conditioning, is a way for you to easily train your cat to do what you desire.

It is a training method that uses a reward system instead of punishment to induce your cat to do as you wish. When you indicate the desired behavior with a click, you reward them with a treat when they repeat the behavior.

The clickers used for training are small plastic devices that create a clicking sound when you press on its metal strip. Unlike your voice, which you cat hears everyday, the click is a distinctive sound that will generate curiosity the first time you use it. When you start training them using the device, they will quickly associate the sound with the behavior that you want them to learn.

Once your cat has associated the click with the behavior you wish them to learn, they will repeat the behavior. It takes patience to train a cat, so don't get flustered if they don't respond the first, or even the second, time you show them what to do.

However, once they have repeated the desired trick or behavior, the treat they receive will help reinforce the positive consequence of their action and your cat will be more amicable to being trained.

Chapter 12 - Clicker Training for Your Cat

You will also want to set goals for using clicker training before you begin. Decide which behaviors need to be replaced, which to encourage and decide if you want to use it to teach your cat some easy tricks. Be reasonable with your goals and prepare to be patient as your train him or her.

First steps in training

The first step to clicker training is getting your cat used to the sound of the clicker. You don't want to randomly use the clicker because you need to associate the sound with a treat in order for the training to work properly.

Click the clicker and immediately give your cat something they love to eat, this will help inspire them to continue to participate in the training. After all, you don't work and expect nothing in return, do you?

Commercial cat treats can be used for their training, but make sure it is something they want to eat. If they don't like the treat, then they will be less likely to cooperate with the training. When you treat them, you can either toss it to them or hand feed them the treat.

Chapter 12 - Clicker Training for Your Cat

Be sure to associate the click with the treat before you begin to redirect their behavior or try to teach them tricks.

Although it can take time for some cats to make the connection between the click and a treat, your Devon Rex is one smart cookie, so it shouldn't take them long at all to learn they will be rewarded for responding to the click. Once they understand that if they respond to the clicker, they will get a treat, you can begin more advanced training.

One of the easiest commands to teach your cat using this trying is to come when they are called. Much like they would respond to the sound of a can opener, if you use the clicker, they will come out of hiding to get their treat. This can be useful when you can't find them and need them to come to you.

Since the Devon is such an intelligent breed, you may be able to teach your cat how to respond to visual and vocal cues. Use the clicker to teach them the command, then associate the visual or vocal cue with the clicker and treat.

Repeat it until you can replace the clicker with the visual or vocal cue, but remember to reward him or her with a treat whenever you use a vocal or visual command, just as you did with the clicker.

It is important to time the clicking with the desired behavior because you want to click during the behavior and not after it. If you click after they start doing the behavior, your cat may abruptly stop what they are doing if they hear the click and expect to be rewarded with a trick. As you work with your cat, he or she should repeat the desired behavior before they get their treat.

Don't

Don't confuse your cat by using multiple clicks. Click once during the behavior and, once they have completed their task, give them their reward. Don't play with the clicker between training sessions either, this will also confuse your cat and they will be disappointed when they don't get a treat after clicks.

Keep the training sessions short so your cat doesn't get bored and you don't get frustrated. As they make small movements toward the goals you've set, reward them for doing so. Treating your cat as it makes progress will let him or her know they are doing the right thing and will repeat it in order to get a yummy treat.

Chapter 12 - Clicker Training for Your Cat

Start training with something easy that your cat is likely to do own its own. If they use their scratching post, nuzzle your hand or sit, click during the act and reward them with a treat. Your Devon Rex will quickly associate that behavior with the click and the treat. Before you know it, he or she will repeat the behavior on command when they hear the click.

The key to clicker training is patience and rewarding your cat. The Devon Rex loves food and they are very smart, which will make them much easier to train than most other cat breeds. Before you know it, you will impress your family and friends with the antics of your well-trained cat.

Chapter 13 - Showing Off Your Devon Rex

Many breeders of purebred cats often strive to produce the best breed of cat that they can and show them at cat shows across the country and, sometimes, around the world. Even if you don't wish to breed your Devon Rex, you may still be interested in placing him or her in a cat show.

Chapter 13 - Showing Off Your Devon Rex

The rules for showing your cat can vary around the world and from show to show, depending on the organization sponsoring the show.

There are several organizations that sponsor cat shows in the United States. The American Association of Cat Enthusiast's (AACE), the Cat Fanciers' Association (CFA), the American Cat Fanciers' Association (ACFA) and The International Cat Association (TICA) are the major organizations that regularly host cat shows in the U.S. and TICA also holds them around the world.

What to do before

Before you decide whether to show your cat, it is a good idea to attend some cat shows to determine if you want to put your cat, as well as yourself, through all of the training that is required. It can take several weeks, if not months, to prepare your cat for show, and if you are new to the circuit attending cat shows will help you understand what types of preparations that you need to make.

A cat that is being shown will need to get used to being handled by judges and spend extended periods of time in pens while waiting at the show. Show cats need to be groomed daily and their claws should be clipped the day before the show. Your cat must be fed well in order to be in good health and maintain the perfect weight for their body structure.

The vaccinations for your cat should be up-to-date or you cannot show them. It is recommended that if your cat's shots are due near the date of the show that you have them vaccinated about 14 days prior to the show in case they have any reactions to the vaccine.

Vaccinations are important because your cat will be in a room with many other cats and you don't want them to get sick from an airborne illness.

To find out when shows are scheduled, you can go online to the organizations' websites to look for their scheduled shows or you can send away for their show schedules. Fill out the entry forms for the shows you wish to place your cat into and give them plenty of time to be processed so nothing goes awry on the day of the show. The entry form should have the closing date for entries on it or you can check with the shows' managers.

Placing your Devon into a cat show will mean that you need to teach your cat to travel well, whether you plan on driving or going by airplane. As you need to train them to stay in a pen for long periods of time, you should be able to easily train them to travel well in a cat carrier.

Chapter 13 - Showing Off Your Devon Rex

If you are driving to cat shows, use a hard-sided carrier with a good latch to secure your cat. For airplane travel, a soft-sided cat carrier would be best.

A cat show is organized into four main classes, which include:

The Kitten Class - Kittens must be at least 14 weeks old before they can be shown, but under 10 months of age.

The Neuter Class - This is a class for altered cats and they are judged by the same breed standards as unaltered cats.

The Open Class - This is open to all breeds in a cat show.

The Household Pet Class - This is open to cats that are altered and of unknown breed origin or who are unregistered. There are no standards used for this class and the cats are judged by their unique qualities.

Your Devon Rex, unless it has been spayed or neutered, it would fit into the Open Class.

When your cat is judged, the judge will physically and visually examine your cat. It will be awarded points based on the breed standard for Devon Rex cats. The maximum number of points that it can be awarded is 100 and the points are based on examining the head, the body and tail, coat, color or markings and your cat's balance.

For the Devon Rex, all colors and markings are considered breed standard. If you are curious about the breed standard for a Devon Rex, the information can be found at the ACFA website:

http://www.acfacat.com/Breed%20Standards/DEVON%20REX.pdf.

Once the judges examine your cat, they will write up a report that is forwarded to the show secretary. The results are recorded and the paperwork is prepared for the "Best in Show" nominations.

A cat can win its breed division and it can also be nominated to win "Best in Show." The cats that have been nominated for "Best in Show" will be taken before a panel of judges, who will re-examine them and then they will vote on which cat to name "Best in Show."

Even if your cat doesn't do well in a show the first time, there are ample opportunities to try again. If you plan to

Chapter 13 - Showing Off Your Devon Rex

show your cat, you must be prepared to spend weeks and months working with them in order to make sure they are ready for the process.

Many people who show cats raise them specifically for that purpose and they may also breed cats. While it can be a lot of work for both you and your cat, it can be a rewarding experience for you and your Devon Rex as well.

Chapter 14 - Traveling with Your Cat

If you do decide to show your cat or if you need to take them on a short trip with you, traveling with a cat can be a challenge. Most cats are not fond of riding in a car, even on short trips to the vet. Although you can try to acclimate them to car travel if you start them off young, some cats never get used to traveling and they do not enjoy the experience.

Unless your Devon Rex has been trained to ride in a car, and likes the experience, then you should transport your cat in a sturdy cat carrier.

You can use either a soft-sided carrier that is made for airplane travel or a hard-sided carrier, which is preferable for car travel. The sturdier carrier will give the cat a little more room to move around since it is a small breed, but, in case of an accident, the carrier will also help protect your cat.

Things to consider

If you are traveling a short distance, you may not need to make any extra preparations when you take your cat with you, but if you are taking a longer trip, you need to bring some essentials along. Traveling with a pet isn't unlike traveling with a child; you need to bring some supplies for them to help make the trip more comfortable and to help keep them calm during it.

Line the carrier with a blanket or towel to give them something soft to cuddle up in, especially if you are traveling when it is cold outside.

Even though a Devon Rex has fur, it is usually thin, so having a blanket or towel will help keep them warm. Take water, food, bowls, a litter pan and litter on the trip with you to accommodate their needs. You also may want to put their favorite small toys in the carrier with them for comfort and so they can keep themselves occupied.

The best place to place the cat carrier is in the middle of the back seat. This will help prevent the sun from shining down on the carrier, which can make the trip uncomfortably warm. When you do sit their carrier on the car seat, use the seat belt to secure the carrier in order to keep it from sliding around if you have to suddenly stop or swerve the car.

If the carrier isn't secured, your cat can be injured if the carrier is accidentally overturned.

Some cats have problems with motion sickness, which can be exacerbated if they can see outside when you're driving. To help prevent your cat getting sick, place their carrier on the floor behind one of the front seats.

Try to prevent the floor air blower from directly blowing onto the carrier and make sure they have a blanket to cuddle up in for summer travel. The air conditioner can make them cold and you will want something they can use for warmth in the carrier with them.

Long distances

On a long trip, you may wish to set up a litter box inside of your vehicle. A covered litter box would work best because it will prevent the litter from spilling onto the floor of your vehicle.

Unlike dogs, your cat shouldn't have to stretch its legs on the trip until you stop for the night. It is very important that you keep your cat in its carrier while traveling, especially when you stop so it doesn't bolt out of the car and get lost in unfamiliar territory.

Airline travel with a pet presents other issues, but the first thing you should do is check with the airline regarding their pet policy before purchasing your ticket. It may be faster to look up airline pet policies online than call each airline, but policies are subject to change and you may wish to call the airline to double check their policy. Most airlines allow you to carry on a pet, so you will probably want to do so for your cat.

Chapter 14 - Traveling with Your Cat

A soft-sided pet carrier fits best under the seat in front of you, unless you wish to go to the expense of buying a ticket for the seat beside you and use a hard-sided carrier.

As you would when traveling in a car, make sure you bring supplies for your cat to make them feel more comfortable. Place a blanket in the carrier so they are kept warm as they travel.

Obtain a health certificate from your vet before traveling by plane because the airline will want to see that your cat has been vaccinated. Carry the health certificate with you at all times so it is easily accessible.

Be sure to put a collar on your cat that has an identification tag with his or her name, your telephone number and address in case something happens and your cat manages to escape its carrier.

If you need to travel internationally, it may be better to have a friend or family member watch your cat while you are gone than try to bring your cat with you. Unless you are going to be moving to another country, making arrangements for a pet can be a hassle for short trips to another country.

Some countries do not permit foreign animals into their country, while others require them to be quarantined upon arrival. It can literally take weeks, if not months, to get approval to bring your pet into another country, so unless you are moving there, try to leave your Devon Rex at home.

Some cats may require a visit to the vet before you take your trip, regardless if it is by car or by plane. They may need to be sedated before you can travel with them if they are really bad travelers or if they get car or air sick. Always check with your veterinarian before giving anything to calm your cat.

While there are some natural herbs you can give cats to help keep them calm, you should never try medicating your cat. Some sedatives or tranquilizers can affect a cat's body temperature and they may have other adverse reactions to them, so it is best to let your vet advise you on the best sedative to give your cat to help it travel better.

Overall

With proper preparation and by bringing the supplies you need with you, you can enjoy traveling with your cat. Work with your Devon and train them to calmly lay in a carrier so they will be used to it when you need to take them on a trip with you.

Start with small trips across town and gradually progress from there in order to get them used to car travel. It may never be their favorite thing to do, but with a little work and preparation, the travel experience will be better for the both of you.

If the female is not bred during estrus, she will go into the interfollicular stage, also called interestrus, which lasts about a week. During this stage, she will show no signs of reproductive activity. She will then go into proestrus and estrus again. If she was mated, but did not get pregnant, the female will go through a stage called metetrus for about 5 to 7 weeks. Again, no signs of reproductive activity will take place.

Chapter 15 - Breeding Your Devon Rex Cats

Even though you may love your Devon Rex and want to breed him or her to produce a litter of kittens, cat breeding isn't something that should be considered lightly.

Chapter 15 - Breeding Your Devon Rex Cats

If you intend to breed your cat, you need to do so responsibly and with a full understanding of what is involved in cat breeding. Doing so for the fun of having kittens in the house or making money from them are poor reasons to get into the business and, all too often, that is why less reputable breeders do so.

Many breeders are motivated to strengthening the Devon Rex breed, not by money. They want to produce stronger offspring that will have less health issues so that the future generations of this breed will live longer, happier lives with their human companions.

These breeders run reputable facilities and will often show their cats in order to introduce their stronger Devons to the cat world.

What to consider

Properly breeding and caring for cats is a time-consuming and expensive undertaking. Before you get into the business, you should talk with other breeders and read everything you can on breeding before you even consider producing a litter of kittens. You will need to learn how to properly care for a pregnant queen, the term used for a female cat that is bred, and properly care for the kittens that are produced, including finding them good homes.

Chapter 15 - Breeding Your Devon Rex Cats

In order to produce the best offspring for the breed, your cat should display excellent breed standards and be healthy in order to breed him or her.

It is important to be committed and involved with the kittens that are produced, preferably for the rest of their lives. It is your responsibility to see that they are prepared for adoption and that they are placed in good homes. There are already too many unwanted kittens in the world and you don't want to add to the population.

Both female and male cats should be allowed to reach maturity before they are bred. For female cats, they can be bred starting at 18 to 24 months of age. If female cats are bred earlier than 18 months of age, they may not have a chance to finish growing, as they will put all of their energy into taking care of and nourishing their kittens.

Male cats should be at least 18 months of age before they are used for breeding. The need to reach maturity in order to make sure they are suitable for breeding as far as their temperament is concerned and to ensure they are healthy.

The male cat's temperament can be passed onto the offspring, just as genetic diseases can be, and you don't want to produce a litter of aggressive or shy kittens if you can prevent that possibility.

Chapter 15 - Breeding Your Devon Rex Cats

If you know you are going to breed your Devons before you adopt them, you should get kittens from unrelated litters to use as the tom and the queen. The Devon Rex breed is an already inner-bred breed and you can further deteriorate the breed if your tom and queen are somehow related.

You don't necessarily need to own both the tom and the queen, but it will make it more convenient for breeding, especially a breed like the Devon that isn't your ordinary cat. A suitable tom may be hard to find, so owning both the tom and queen may be more convenient for you.

Before breeding

Before you commence breeding, you need to have your veterinarian give your cats a thorough examination, check their stools for parasites and make sure that their vaccinations are up-to-date. You want your cats as healthy as possible before producing a litter of kittens because any illness or disease they have can be passed on to their offspring. They should also be free of ear mites, ringworm and fleas.

Both parents need to be tested and certified that they are free from the feline leukemia virus (FeLV) and feline immunodeficiency virus (FIV).

Chapter 15 - Breeding Your Devon Rex Cats

Have your cats tested for the genetic diseases the Devon Rex are known to have, such as patella luxation, myopathy, spastic and hip dysplasia. A responsible breeder will not use their cats for breeding if they test positive for any of these conditions and will spay or neuter them instead.

It is important for female cats to be at their ideal weight before they conceive. If they are too thin or too heavy, they can have problems getting pregnant, carrying a litter and queening, which is the act of giving birth. By feeding them a proper diet, you can keep both your female and male cats in good health and at their ideal weight throughout their lives.

Along with your cats' physical health, their temperaments or personalities need to also be considered before they are bred. Kittens can inherit their parents' personalities, so your cats' personalities should be checked before breeding.

Cats that are aggressive or shy can produce kittens with those traits, which are considered undesirable traits for many owners. Cats that are laid-back and friendly will be more likely to produce kittens that are easy going and friendly.

If you do adopt Devon Rex cats with the idea that you will breed them, select your male and female very carefully. Make sure they are healthy and have been well taken care of, which will help ensure that you produce healthy kittens.

Check their medical certifications, get to know their personalities and adopt cats with the best breed standard that you can. If you are careful in selecting your male and female cats, you will be more likely to produce a healthy, friendly litter of Devon Rex kittens.

Chapter 16 - Caring for the Queen During Pregnancy

Once your male and female Devon Rex are at least 18 months of age, they are ready to be bred. The queen, your female cat, will go into heat during certain seasons of the year, which is called seasonally polyestrous.

Chapter 16 - Caring for the Queen During Pregnancy

If females are not bred, they will cycle many times. Cats also need to breed before they ovulate, they are reflex ovulators. Indoor cats, which are exposed to artificial light, can cycle year-round, while outdoor cats usually cycle in the spring and summer months.

There are five stages to a cat's heat, or estrous, cycle: anestrus, proestrus, estrus, the interfollicular stage and metestrus. The anestrus stage usually occurs during the winter months and the tom is not interested in the queen during this stage nor is the queen attracted to the tom.

The proestrus stage occurs just before the female goes into heat. During this time, she may "call" to the tom, roll around and/or rub on the ground.

However, she usually will not allow the tom to come near her yet. Female cats do not bleed during this stage as other animals, such as dogs, do. The proestrus stage can progress to the estrus stage in just a few hours. The estrus stage is when a female is in heat.

The estrus stage will last for about a week and the queen should be taken to the tom for mating, if you do not also own the tom. It is at this time that the queen will allow a tom to approach and mate with her.

Chapter 16 - Caring for the Queen During Pregnancy

Mating

When they do mate, it will last anywhere from 1 to 20 seconds and the tom will need to have an escape route away from the queen, who will often respond aggressively after mating. Use a box or make sure there is a shelf nearby that the tom can jump into or onto immediately after mating with the queen.

You will know that the queen has mated by her actions immediately afterwards. She will thoroughly groom herself and not be approachable for about an hour after she mates.

Afterwards, the tom can once again approach her and they will resume mating. To help ensure that she gets pregnant, you can allow your female to mate three times a day for the first three days of estrus. Studies have shown that this helps produce ovulation in 90% of queens.

If she was mated successfully, she will be pregnant for 63 days and you can determine her due date by adding 63 days to each day she was bred.

However, if for some reason she aborts or loses her nursing kittens, the queen will return to the estrus stage within two to three weeks. She will then be ready to be bred again, if you so desire.

Chapter 16 - Caring for the Queen During Pregnancy

First signs

The first signs of pregnancy are the lack of heat cycles. It is usually difficult to tell if a queen is pregnant during the first two to three weeks of her pregnancy. Several methods can be used to determine if the queen is pregnant.

An ultrasound can be done to check for fetuses at days 14 or 15, your veterinarian will be able to feel the fetuses with abdominal palpations around days 17 or 18 and heartbeats using an ultrasound are detectable starting around day 24.

The most accurate method for determining a pregnancy is to have the queen x-rayed around days 43 to 45, when the fetuses' skeletons may be seen, but the later the x-rays are done, the more accurate they will be.

You won't notice anything physically until about the 5th week of pregnancy when the queen's abdomen starts to enlarge, but if she has a small litter, it will take longer for her to show.

What to do when she is pregnant

Once the pregnancy has been confirmed, you should start the queen on a vitamin and mineral supplement prescribed by your vet. Your vet can help you make sure that the food you are feeding your cat and the supplement she is given will provide a well balanced diet.

Be careful not to over supplement as this can adversely affect the developing kittens. Your cat should also be allowed to exercise normally as this will keep her from gaining too much weight and help her maintain her muscle tone.

If she was on a premium cat food before her pregnancy, you should maintain that diet for the first few weeks of her pregnancy. You can read more about cat nutrition in a following chapter. At about the fourth week of pregnancy, you will want to add a high-quality kitten food to her diet.

Each week you will increase the amount of kitten food to her diet until the final week, when she should be eating nothing but kitten food. This will help provide all of the essential vitamins and minerals that the kittens will need to be at their healthiest when they are born.

It is a good idea to increase the queen's meal frequency to three times a day by the middle of her pregnancy, around day 30, you can allow her to free feed during this time.

During the last week of pregnancy, she may need to eat small meals every three to four hours as the kittens continue to grow. Kittens grow the most during the last two weeks of gestation.

Chapter 16 - Caring for the Queen During Pregnancy

During the last week of her pregnancy, as well as the first three to four weeks of lactating, you can increase the amount of food she eats. It can be increased one and a half to twice the amount of food she ate before she became pregnant.

As long as she maintains a healthy weight during lactation, the queen should be able to have the extra food and she will need it in order to keep up her own energy levels and properly nourish her kittens.

Medications

If possible, all medications should be avoided while the queen is pregnant or lactating. The only time medications harmful to the developing fetuses should be administered to the queen is in order to save her life.

For any other medications or supplements, consult with your veterinarian before you give them to the queen to see if they will be harmful to her kittens.

Just before the due date

You will want to set up a nesting box for the queen about two weeks before her due date. Something as simple as a cardboard box or a laundry basket works well for a nesting box. Just line them with a blanket or towels to create a soft area for the queen and her kittens. Setting it up in advance will allow the queen to become accustomed to the nesting area before she goes into labor.

If you want to be present during labor, start taking the queen's temperature about two weeks before her due date. Lubricate the thermometer with margarine or KY jelly so it is easy to insert into the rectum. Insert it approximately half an inch and let it remain there for three minutes. More than likely the cat will not be too pleased with this treatment and you will have to hold the thermometer in place while someone else holds the cat still.

The temperature should read between 101 and 102 degrees Fahrenheit during, but her temperature will drop to 100 degrees just before she goes into labor. When her temperature does drop, the queen should deliver her litter within 24 hours. There are other signs of impending labor that will start taking place within 24 to 48 hours before she goes into labor.

She may seem anxious, restless and start looking for a place to have her litter. When she starts this behavior, confine her to the room you where you want her to have the kittens.

The room should be darkened and in a quiet area of your home in order to make her feel it is safe enough for her kittens. Make sure she has access to fresh water, food and a clean litter box at all times.

Labor

Just before she begins labor, the queen may also start to repeatedly lick her abdomen and vagina. She may have a discharge prior to birth, but you probably won't see it as she will lick it away. She will be dilating at this time, but you won't see any outward signs of it. Don't check the area just leave her alone during this time.

Her breathing may increase, and she may yowl or pace about while she is in labor. As contractions begin, the queen will lie on her side, then get up and squat while pressing downward to drop her kittens.

You can watch from a distance, but don't interrupt or disturb her while she is in the process of having her kittens. You should see the first kitten emerge about an hour after her labor begins.

Labor may only last a few minutes before the first kitten arrives and the next one will arrive within 10 minutes to an hour later. The remaining kittens will arrive within the same intervals. They come out wrapped in a membrane, so the queen will immediately start licking her kitten to open the sac and allow the kitten to breathe. The licking also helps to stimulate the kitten's circulation and respiration.

If she cannot break through the sac or doesn't do so, you will need to gently, but vigorously rub the kitten using a soft towel to get the membrane off it and allow them to breathe.

Place the kitten at a nipple because the queen will immediately start nursing her kittens after chewing away the umbilical cord and before the rest of her litter arrives. Nursing the kitten will help stimulate further contractions.

You may need to help cut any umbilical cords the queen has forgotten to take care of herself. Gently tie a string or piece of dental floss around the kitten's umbilical cord and snip it about an inch long. It usually takes two to six hours for her entire litter to be delivered, if it takes longer than seven hours, gather her and the kittens and take her to the vet.

Just after

Once she has finished having her litter, you can quietly clean up after her. Place her food and water nearby because she will not want to leave her kittens unattended for too long the first day or two. Leave her in the birthing room, keeping it darkened and quiet so as not to disturb the new family. If you take good care of the queen before and

Chapter 16 - Caring for the Queen During Pregnancy

during her pregnancy, as well as labor, she will be more like to have a healthy litter of kittens.

Chapter 17 - Raising Healthy, Happy Kittens

After the kittens have arrived, the real work has begun. Even though there may not be much you can do for the kittens during the first few days, the queen will see to most of their care, you can ensure that the room they are in stays warm enough for them.

Body temperature

Kittens cannot regulate their body temperature for the first few weeks of their lives and the room should stay around 75 to 80 degrees Fahrenheit for the first week, then you can gradually drop it to 70 degrees.

If you need to use a heat source in the room, do not make it warmer than the queen as the kittens will gravitate toward it in order to nurse. Kittens usually lay on the sides or atop their littermates to stay warm and to have contact with them. If they spread out, they are probably too warm.

A kitten's normal temperature is around 97 degrees Fahrenheit and it will gradually climb each week until it reaches 100.5 to 102.5, which is the same as an adult cat, at around four weeks of age.

Food

In order to keep the queen well fed so she can keep her kittens nourished, keep her food, water and a litter box nearby. She will not want to leave her kittens for very long and she will need an almost constant supply of high-quality kitten food to eat in order to keep up with the feeding demands of her kittens.

The queen's appetite will increase by double that of her pre-pregnancy feedings and she should be allowed to free feed. Monitor how much she eats, drinks and uses the restroom to make sure she stays healthy.

What to look out for

A healthy kitten is easy to spot as they are plump, have a firm body and they are vigorous. They will nurse about every one to two hours and they will nurse until their tiny stomachs appear rounded and they sleep quietly.

If you see them moving around a lot and crying, they may not be getting enough to eat. Swallowing air can make their stomachs appear rounded just as it would if they were feeding normally. As they weaken, they will stop moving around and crying.

If some of the kittens appear not to be feeding well or not getting enough to eat, take the queen and the kittens in to see your veterinarian. You may need to intercede and hand feed a kitten that is having trouble nursing or isn't getting enough to eat. Kittens that are not thriving should be taken in to see your vet as well in order to diagnose any genetic disease or birth defects. Some defects, like cleft palate, are not compatible with life and they will be euthanized humanely.

Weight

A Devon Rex kitten normally weighs between 90 and 100 grams at birth and those weighing under 90 grams many expire within a few days after their birth. Although kittens may lose a small amount of weight about 24 hours after their birth, the normal weight gain is between 7 to 10 grams per day.

Their weight should double within the first 14 days of their life. It is important to weigh new kittens every day for their first two weeks and then two to three times a week until they have been weaned. One of the signs of illness is a kitten's failure to gain weight.

Nursing

When they are nursing, you may notice that the kittens are at the same teat each time they fed. Kittens prefer to use the same teat each time they nurse, which they will pick out during the first few days of life. They will use their sense of smell to find their preferred teat when it is time for them to eat.

Chapter 17 - Raising Healthy, Happy Kittens

While they are nursing, the queen will lick their stomachs and perineal area to stimulate their ability to urinate and defecate. She will continue to do this for the first two to three weeks of their life.

You should check the queen's mammary glands and nipples at least once a day to check for redness, hardness, streaking color or discharge.

An infection of a mammary gland, called mastitis, needs to be treated immediately. Sometimes the infection can be milked out and using hot compresses on the area will help prevent the infection from spreading. Antibiotics could be necessary as well. If there is mastitis in several glands, the kittens may need to be hand fed.

Growth stages

Grooming the kittens starts at an early age, as their little claws will need to be trimmed to keep them from scratching the queen's mammary glands. Their nails should be trimmed starting within a few days of their birth and maintained weekly. This will also help them get used to the process of nail trimming, making it much easier to do as they get older.

Chapter 17 - Raising Healthy, Happy Kittens

Kittens are born without teeth and their baby teeth, the deciduous teeth, will start coming in at about two to four weeks of age. Around the second week of life, you will also want to check the queen's mammary glands for bite marks as well as scratches.

By the time a kitten is eight weeks of age, all of their deciduous teeth should be present. Kittens will eventually lose their deciduous teeth, which will be replaced with adult teeth.

At around three to four weeks of age, the kittens will start imitating the queen when she eats and drinks. You need to keep a shallow bowl of water out for them for at least part of the day so they have access to water.

At around this time, you can start making and feeding them kitten mush. Kitten mush is a blend of high quality kitten food, replacement kitten milk and hot water. Blend it until it has the same consistency of human baby cereal.

The kittens should be fed kitten mush three to four times a day at first. Once they have checked out the kitten mush and eaten some of it, the queen should be allowed to finish it and clean her kittens.

Each week, decrease the replacement milk and water in the mush and blend it less. By the time they are 7 to 8 weeks of age, they should be eating dry kitten food and they should be fully weaned off the teat as well.

Keep the nesting box clean by changing it out at least once a day as the kittens will be urinating and defecating in it for the first several weeks of life.

At around four weeks old, they will start behavior that looks as if they are scratching at sand. They will start following the queen to the litter box and, while they may just play in it at first, at around six weeks of age, they will be learning to use it for urinating and defecating. They will learn how to bury their feces from watching the queen and they will need access to a litter pan with shorter sides in order to be able to climb in and out of it.

As she starts to spend more time away from her kittens, they will start to follow the queen from the nesting box to explore their world. It is important to supervise them as they explore so they aren't lost or injured.

Make sure they have soft toys available to play with and, if they fall asleep in odd spots, return them to the box to rest. The queen may take care of that herself, but it never hurts to lend a helping hand.

Chapter 17 - Raising Healthy, Happy Kittens

Socialization

The kittens will start going through a socialization period beginning somewhere between two to seven weeks of age. This is when you need to begin working with them so they are not frightened by loud noises, car rides, allow them to have more human contact, including children, and start introducing them to any other pets that you have in the house.

If you have any other litters around the same age, set up a "play date" where you can introduce the kittens and supervise their interactions.

Expose them to normal household sounds and don't worry about being quiet during the day, they need to get used to the noise in order to develop into unafraid adults.

Handle them for about 30 to 40 minutes a day between the ages of two to seven weeks of age. Pet them, play with them and talk with them as you interact with the kittens. By the time they are 12 weeks old they should be fully socialized.

For the most part, kittens learn from the queen by imitating her actions. That is how they learn how to eat, how to use the litter box, hunt and they learn to fear what she fears. Since the Devon Rex breed is generally friendly, fearless

Chapter 17 - Raising Healthy, Happy Kittens

and fun loving, you can expect the kittens to turn out the same way.

Chapter 18 - Finding Forever Homes for Kittens (and tips if you are buying from a breeder)

As a responsible breeder, one of the most important things
you can do for your Devon Rex kittens is to ensure that
they go to a good home. As you care for them and watch
them grow, you will soon be able to determine their
personalities, which will help you place them in the right
environment.

Observe them during playtime, eating and sleeping to get a
good idea of their individual temperaments. Becoming

Chapter 18 - Finding Forever Homes for Kittens (and tips if you are buying from a breeder)

familiar with the kittens will help you find them a good forever home that is loving and nurturing.

When you start allowing people in to interact with the kittens to see which one they want to adopt, you will be able to match the people with the kitten by their temperaments.

Prospective owners that live close to you may want to make several visits before deciding on which kitten to adopt. Have them bring the entire family in to look at the kittens so you can better match up kittens to owners. If there are children in the family, it is important to see how well the children will handle the kitten. If you feel a prospective owner isn't right for one of your kittens, turn them down. Your first responsibility is to your kittens.

As they are looking at, deciding which kitten they want, and evaluating you as a breeder, you should be evaluating the prospective owners as well.

Don't be shy about asking them questions about their desires in adopting a kitten and their experience with owning pets. Some people may find the questions intrusive, but you are only asking so you can match them up with the best kitten for them and to make sure your kittens go to good homes.

Chapter 18 - Finding Forever Homes for Kittens (and tips if you are buying from a breeder)

Ask them if they know anything about the Devon Rex breed, if they plan to breed the kitten or show them. Find out if someone will be home during the day with the kitten or if everyone is at work or school.

Although a kitten doesn't require as much work as a puppy, they still need attention, affection and companionship. If you feel it will be a good home for your Devon kittens, you might suggest a pair of kittens to keep each other occupied when they are alone if there are no other pets in the family.

Usually, a kitten should not go home on the same day that a family visits their kitten for the first time. The only exception may be if the adoptive family is traveling to pick up their kitten.

Most kittens are ready to go home with their adoptive family by the time they are 12 weeks old, but some breeders like to keep them up to 16 weeks or four months old. This allows them to be fully socialized and given some preliminary training. It also allows the breeder plenty of time to find their kittens good homes.

Make sure the adoptive person or family agrees to the terms of the contract before you present it for them to sign. The contract will state exactly which kitten they are adopting, its date of birth, the price they are paying, his or her parents' names and numbers, the date of sale and both the breeder's and the buyer's contact information. The contract will also state when the kitten will be released to its new owner and when it should be spayed or neutered.

Show them the medical certifications that you have on the parents and kittens, their updated vaccination information and include copies of them, plus medical records in with the contract that you give the adoptive family or person. Put in the contract that if they are unable to keep the kitten, that you get the first chance at getting the kitten back and state in the contract if you will give them a full, partial or any refund at all.

If you get to know the prospective owners, not only will you be able to match them up with a kitten, but you will be able to tell if they have a home good enough for one of your kittens.

If you like, you can stipulate in the contract whether the kitten is to stay indoors, be allowed outside and whether they are allowed to declaw the kitten. If you find out they broke the stipulations of the contract at anytime, you may be able to get the kitten back into your care.

If you need a contract there are lots freely available online if

Chapter 18 - Finding Forever Homes for Kittens (and tips if you are buying from a breeder)

you search Google for terms like 'cat adoption contract template'

Encourage them to take the kitten to their vet within the first 48 to 72 hours of ownership and, after the kitten goes to its new home, check in with the adoptive family two to three days later.

Some breeders keep in touch with the families throughout the cat's life and you may wish to do the same to ensure you have chosen a good environment for your Devon Rex kittens. Making sure they have a great forever home is one of your greatest responsibilities as a breeder.

Conclusion

Thank you again for buying this book! I spent months writing it. As someone who has loved these cats for years, friends told me to share my knowledge!

I hope this book helped you decide if the Devon Rex breed is right for your home and to learn how to raise it properly.

Please Help....

Finally, if you enjoyed this book, please, please, please take the time to share your thoughts and post a review on whatever site you purchased it from. It will be greatly appreciated!

The biggest criticism is always going to be making a book specific to the 'Devon Rex' I have tried where possible to show you how this breed is unique and why it is different. But equally it does share similarities with other breeds.

Index

car, 42, 72, 89, 90, 91, 92, 93, 118

carrier, 42, 59, 84, 89, 90, 91, 92, 93

cat bed, 71

Cat Fanciers' Association, 83

cat show, 82, 84, 85

cat shows, 11, 82, 83, 85

cat tree, 23, 24, 46, 53, 73

catteries, 13, 14, 15

certificate, 92

certifications, 100, 123

certified, 16, 39, 98

CFA, 83

chew, 52, 63

chewing, 49, 52, 63, 109

children, 13, 118, 121

Children, 45

claws, 24, 27, 28, 53, 65, 73, 83, 115

Clicker, 76

colors, 10, 86

comfort, 63, 64, 90

companionship, 6, 45, 122

constipated, 51

contract, 122, 123

cooing, 44, 46

Cornish Rex, 8, 9, 26

costs, 41, 70

cuddle, 45, 47, 69, 90, 91

cuddling, 63

curious, 13, 67, 73, 86

curly, 8, 9, 11, 26

declawing, 53

Dental, 74

depression, 53, 55, 60

Devon, 6, 7, 8, 9, 10, 11, 12, 13, 14, 15, 16, 17, 18, 19, 22, 24, 25, 26, 27, 30, 31, 32, 33, 34, 35, 38, 40, 41, 42, 43, 44, 45, 46, 47, 48, 49, 50, 52, 53, 56, 57, 59, 67, 69, 70, 71, 73, 75, 76, 79, 81, 82, 84, 85, 86, 87, 89, 90, 93, 95, 96, 98, 99, 101, 118, 120, 122, 124, 125

Devon Rex Breed Club, 14

dewormed, 17, 20

diet, 22, 23, 36, 52, 99, 105

disasters, 59

disease, 16, 20, 28, 31, 33, 72, 98, 113

diseases, 16, 31, 34, 38, 97, 99

dog, 44, 69

dogs, 17, 32, 40, 45, 59, 72,

Kitten mush, 116

kittens, 8, 9, 10, 11, 13, 15, 16, 17, 18, 19, 23, 26, 28, 29, 34, 52, 70, 95, 96, 97, 98, 99, 100, 103, 105, 106, 107, 108, 109, 111, 112, 113, 114, 115, 116, 117, 118, 120, 121, 122, 123, 124

labor, 107, 108, 110

leukemia, 20, 98

lick, 62, 108, 115

licking, 62, 63, 108

limping, 33

litter, 8, 10, 20, 23, 49, 50, 51, 58, 59, 71, 90, 91, 95, 96, 97, 98, 99, 100, 104, 107, 109, 112, 117, 118

loyalty, 44

male, 8, 9, 71, 97, 99, 101

mammary glands, 115, 116

mating, 102, 103

meat, 45

medical, 31, 35, 57, 62, 71, 100, 123

medications, 106

meowing, 49, 50, 67

milk, 29, 46, 116

molting, 11

motion sickness, 90

Ms. Cox, 8

nail clipper, 27

nails, 25, 27, 115

nerves, 27

nesting, 106, 117

neuter, 71, 99

Neuter Class, 85

noises, 59, 118

nursing, 103, 109, 113, 114

OCD, 55, 60, 61, 63

odor, 52

Open Class, 85

organizations, 83, 84

owners, 7, 14, 24, 39, 44, 69, 73, 99, 121, 123

parents, 16, 98, 99, 123

patella luxation, 32, 33, 99

Patience, 58

patient, 60, 78

patterns, 10

people, 10, 13, 14, 17, 22, 41, 43, 49, 66, 69, 70, 73, 76, 87, 121

personality, 6, 43, 46, 48, 49, 56

pixie, 6, 10

TICA, 83

time, 6, 18, 19, 20, 21, 22, 24, 29, 32, 37, 39, 42, 44, 51, 56, 57, 62, 66, 69, 75, 77, 79, 80, 84, 86, 96, 102, 105, 106, 108, 114, 116, 117, 118, 122, 125

toilet, 20, 21

Tooth decay, 28

toxic, 46

toxins, 46

toys, 13, 20, 23, 46, 52, 58, 71, 90, 117

train, 29, 44, 76, 77, 78, 81, 84, 93

trained, 38, 76, 77, 81, 89

training, 28, 76, 77, 78, 79, 80, 81, 83, 122

travel, 42, 84, 89, 91, 92, 93

traveling, 42, 88, 89, 90, 91, 92, 93, 122

Traveling, 88, 89

trick, 76, 77, 80

tricks, 44, 76, 78, 79

trust, 37, 65, 66

ultrasound, 40, 104

umbilical cords, 109

United States, 12, 83

urinary tract, 51

urine, 51, 71

vet, 30, 36, 37, 38, 39, 40, 41, 42, 57, 63, 71, 89, 92, 93, 104, 109, 113, 124

veterinarian, 16, 17, 28, 29, 34, 37, 38, 40, 41, 42, 51, 54, 56, 57, 63, 74, 93, 98, 104, 106, 113

veterinarians, 37, 38, 39

vocalization, 50

voice, 50, 58, 64, 77

Von Willebrand Disease, 32

water, 20, 22, 26, 52, 53, 58, 59, 74, 90, 108, 109, 112, 116

weaned, 19, 114, 117

weigh, 9, 114

winking, 66

x-rays, 40, 104